At Least A Mill[ion]
Tavra Imagines Her Possibilities

Written by Arvat McClaine
Illustrated by Isabella Millet

Dedication:

To my mom who always told me, "Where there is a will, there is a way."

To my hubby whose imagination is so huge, that it causes me to live in a perpetual fairy-tale.

To everyone who dreams the "impossible" dream and keeps our world expanding in the most magnificent ways!

Published by Parker & Co., LLC
P.O. Box 50040
Richmond, VA 23250

ISBN: (paperback): 978-1-952733-34-5
ISBN: (hardback): 978-1-952733-35-2
ISBN: (ebook): 978-1-952733-36-9

"I know I can run faster than this. It's time for me to pick up my speed," Tavra thought as she ran as fast as she could in the race against her classmates.

Tavra didn't even know that she liked to run, but when her teacher, Mrs. Hicks, said, "On your mark! Get set! GO!" something stirred up in Tavra that made her want to run. And, she wanted to win!

1

As her determination grew, it seemed like she also grew wings on her feet. She passed Jaden, then Zari, then Ayana. Right in front of her were Ricky and Jamal. She imagined herself switching into a higher gear as she struggled to catch up with them, too.

"I know I can catch them," she thought. "Just push a little harder."

Soon enough, she was passing them, too.

Tavra noticed that it was getting harder and harder for her to breathe, but Lauren was still in front of her.

"I must keep going," Tavra thought.

Before she knew it, she could see the finish line right up ahead. She was happy that the race was almost over, but she didn't know if she was going to catch Lauren in time.

"Go, Lauren!" Tavra could hear some of her classmates shout.

4

"Tavra, you can catch her! Push!" she heard
other classmates shout.

So, that's what Tavra did. She pushed.

And, right at the finish line, she caught Lauren.

"Who won the race?" everyone asked. No one
was quite sure.

Tavra said a little prayer and hoped that she would be the winner. But Lauren was over there doing the same thing—praying that she was the winner.

"Well, that was a great battle to the finish," Mrs. Hicks said. "The winner is... Tavra! Tavra, you will represent us against the other classroom winners!"

6

Tavra was very pleased with herself, and rather than walk home from school like she usually did, she decided to run!

"Mama, guess what?" Tavra said.

"What?" her mom asked.

"I won the race at school today!" Tavra exclaimed.

"You did what? I didn't even know you liked to run!" her mom said with surprise.

"Me either, Mama! But, as soon as Mrs. Hicks said, 'GO!' I just knew that I wanted to win! So, I pushed and pushed! I flew past everyone!" Tavra said.

"Well, I am very proud of you for pushing for something that you really wanted. Congratulations!" her mom said.

"Now, I am going to represent our class against the fastest runners in the entire school!" Tavra said.

9

"That's awesome, Tavra! When is that race?" her mom asked.

"In 2 weeks. So, I have to start practicing now!" Tavra said.

For the next several days, Tavra ran to
school in the mornings. She ran around
the playground at recess, and she ran
home from school in the afternoons.

11

On one of her runs home, Tavra saw Jamal, Ricky, and Tareq, her three friends from school, playing football on the sidewalk up ahead of her. Ricky ran backwards towards Tavra, preparing for the catch that Jamal had thrown. Tavra slowed her pace slightly just to be certain that she would not get hit by the ball. But Ricky made the perfect catch.

Suddenly, Ricky turned towards Tavra in an attempt to run. The two of them crashed right into each other! Bam!

And they both fell to the ground!

"Ouch!" they both exclaimed, stunned as they laid on the ground.

14

Jamal and Tareq laughed as they helped Tavra and Ricky to their feet.

"It's not funny," Tavra pouted as she realized her ankle was hurting from the fall.

"Aww, you will be okay," Jamal said as he helped Tavra gather her belongings that were on the ground.

16

Tavra turned to leave. "Ouch!" she said, as a shot of pain went through her ankle. She began a slow hobble home.

"Oh, no! I can barely walk. How am I going to run?!" she thought.

Tavra made it home, but by now, she didn't know if she was more mad or sad.

"Tavra, what happened?" her mom asked as Tavra began hopping on one leg.

"Ricky ran into me and knocked me down! Now, my ankle hurts and I won't be able to run in the race next week," Tavra pouted.

"Okay, calm down, Tavra. Let's take a look at your ankle," her mom said. "Let me prop your ankle up on some pillows and put some ice on it. That should help. You may need to stay off of it for a few days. That means no running on it, Tavra!" her mom said.

20

"But, Mama, I have to practice for my race!" Tavra said.

"I mean it, Tavra. No running on it until there is no more pain. I am sure it will be better in time for the race," her mom said.

Tavra remained quiet for the rest of the evening, allowing her ankle to rest. But she still had all kinds of thoughts playing in her head over and over again.

"I probably won't even be able to run on race day now. But, even if I feel better on race day, I can't practice between now and then, so I know I won't be able to win. I'm so mad at that Ricky for knocking me down."

Tavra, still mad and still sad, began drifting off to sleep.

But, tonight, she had a visitor.

It was Princess Vati, that same beautiful princess Tavra had seen before. It seemed that there was a spotlight on the inside of her because she glowed so brightly. She looked a lot like Tavra, only slightly older.

"Greetings, Tavra!" Princess Vati said.

"Hello! You came to see me again," Tavra said, sounding a little surprised.

"Yes, Tavra. I told you that I am never far away. I am always watching and whispering loving words into your ear," Princess Vati said.

24

"So, I guess you heard? I hurt my ankle. Now, I may not be able to run in my race next week. And even if I am healed by then, I still can't practice this week!" Tavra said.

"Yes, Tavra, I heard," Princess Vati said.

25

"I'm so mad at that Ricky! Why can't he watch where he is going? Because of him, I'm not going to be able to win that race!" Tavra said.

"Tavra, do you remember what I told you about saving yourself?" Princess Vati asked.

"Saving myself? What does that have to do with this?" Tavra asked. "My ankle is hurt and there is nothing I can do about it except lay here with my foot propped up."

With a wave of her wand, Princess Vati and Tavra went sailing up to the fluffiest cloud they could find.

"Saving yourself means you have to focus on what you DO want instead of focusing on what you DON'T want," Princess Vati said.

27

"Well, I want to show up and do my best. I want to win. But I don't see how because now I can't even practice," Tavra said, enjoying the view from the cloud.

"Tavra, there is more than one way to do everything. You are connected to God, who creates all things. And, God has at least a million ways to get anything done. All you have to do is to go into your imagination and pick out one!" Princess Vati glowed more brightly as she spoke.

"I don't understand what you mean. I wanted to practice my running every day. But, now I can't," Tavra said.

"Oh, but you can," Princess Vati explained. "You can use your *imagination*. In your imagination, you can run faster and further and have more fun than ever before."

"I guess I could. But that won't help me on race day," Tavra said.

"Oh, but it will, Tavra. The best athletes in the world use their imaginations to see themselves going faster and harder and longer. They see themselves winning. And you can do this, too, Tavra. Practice seeing, feeling, and believing what you want in your mind," Princess Vati said.

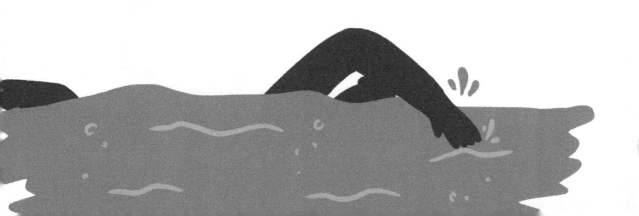

30

So, if I want to win the race, instead of practicing running, I have to practice *feeling* like I am running. I have to *imagine* myself running fast and *see* myself winning the medal?" Tavra asked.

"Yes, Tavra. And, most importantly, you have to have fun while you are doing it! Make your imagination as colorful and joyful as you can!" Princess Vati said.

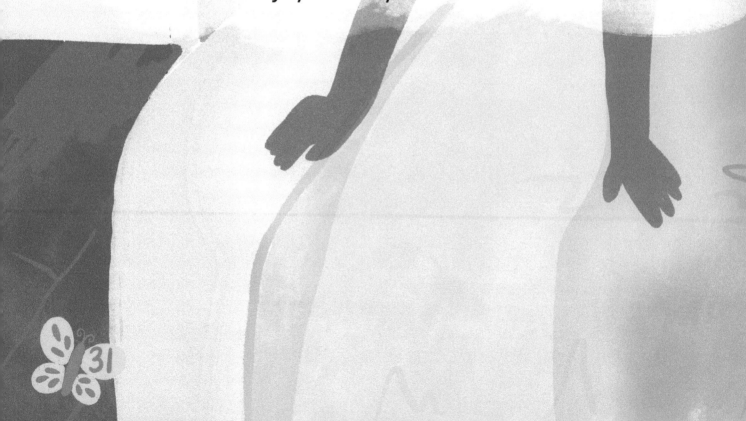

"Okay, I will," Tavra said, realizing that she was back in her room as she drifted off into a deep sleep.

Upon awakening, Tavra remembered what her visitor told her. Focus on what you DO want. Use your imagination to see and feel what you want over and over again. And make it fun!

"On your mark. Get set. Go!" In her mind, Tavra took off running at her top speed. Her nearest competitor was a beautiful, black stallion with a rainbow–colored mane and tail! "Oh, my, he is so pretty," she thought, as she remembered to shift into a higher gear so that she could catch up with the dazzling horse. The faster she ran, the faster the horse galloped, but she managed to run right past him.

33

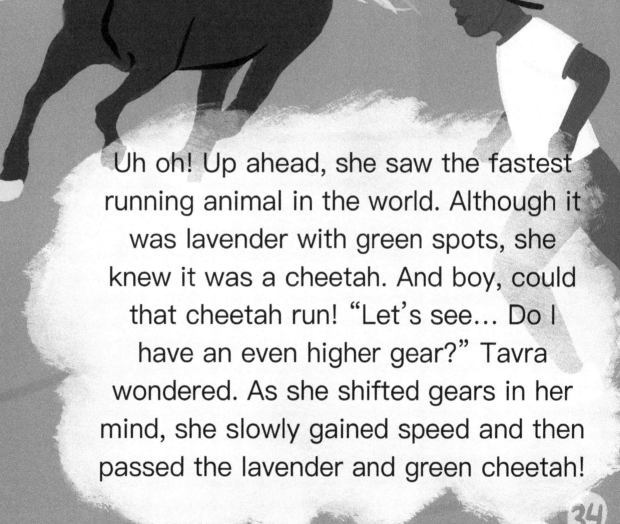

Uh oh! Up ahead, she saw the fastest running animal in the world. Although it was lavender with green spots, she knew it was a cheetah. And boy, could that cheetah run! "Let's see… Do I have an even higher gear?" Tavra wondered. As she shifted gears in her mind, she slowly gained speed and then passed the lavender and green cheetah!

34

"Well, that was the fastest running animal on Earth, and I just passed her! So, now, I am the fastest," Tavra said, relaxing just a little.

"Don't forget about me," Tavra heard a voice singing from up above.

35

"A pink eagle? No one said I would be racing against a bird!" Tavra thought. Even in her imagination, Tavra couldn't outrun the pink bird. "Wait," Tavra thought. "This is MY imagination! I can grow wings!" Suddenly, wings sprouted from Tavra's back. It was exactly what she needed because she literally flew past the pink eagle and right to the finish line.

"I won! I won!" Tavra exclaimed as she saw herself receiving the gold medal.

Tavra practiced that story so many times in her imagination that on race day, she was not worried at all. She knew she was going to go out there, do her best, and have the time of her life.

Author's Bio:

Arvat McClaine, best-selling author of *Through Her Own Eyes—Tavra's Journey to Self-Love,* is a world-traveler and has spoken internationally about how to move from a life of struggle to one where your biggest dreams come true. Arvat co-founded the first independent African-centered school in the state of Virginia (pre-K-8th grade), and has worked extensively with both children and adults in the fields of mental health and personal development.

Arvat literally married "the boy next door." She and her husband, Harry Watkins, have been best friends for about 40 years. They are both avid entrepreneurs and adventurers, having traveled to all 7 continents, jumped out of an airplane, and climbed Mt. Kilimanjaro together. Additionally, Arvat has walked barefoot across a hot bed of coals and is an endurance athlete. Her greatest passion is igniting the "magic" that we all have within to live our best lives.